How the Firefly got its light

The Adventurous Tale of Jugnu Rani

By
Pradyumna Kumar

Translated from Hindi by
Urvashi Butalia

Mapin Publishing

Once upon a time, Trees and People were friends.

They cared very deeply for each other. Trees had feet and could also walk, just like People. You would see Trees and People dancing and singing together. Their children would play together merrily.

Jugnu Rani, the smallest of Fireflies, loved this friendship.

But she felt very bad when she looked at herself. **"Why is my body so small?"** she wondered. "Had I been a little bigger, I could have played games with Trees and People. How I wish I could join them in singing songs. But, I am small and so alone. What can I do?" She would think this and become sad.

One such day, Jugnu spotted a group of Honeybees. She saw that Rani Madhumakhi, the queen-bee, was sitting on a flower. Jugnu quickly flew to her and asked, **"Rani Madhumakhi, what are you doing? Why are you sitting on these flowers?"**

"I am doing something very useful. I'm collecting nectar from these Flowers," replied Rani Madhumakhi happily. "I'll make honey from it. People love honey. I will also eat the honey, just like other Honeybees. When I take nectar from these Flowers, it helps the Plants."

Although Jugnu was pleased with Rani Madhumakhi's efforts, she thought to herself, **"If only I could also do something useful..."**

Suraj Dada advises Jugnu

Feeling sad again, Jugnu looked up at the blue sky. What did she see there? The sky was filled with hundreds of Birds flying around freely.

She decided to join them and fly away, hoping she would find something useful to do. When she was quite high up in the sky, she saw a ball of fire. She went close to it only to realize it was not a fire-ball but her beloved friend Suraj Dada, the sun!

Suraj Dada saw Jugnu's sad face. He asked her, "Why is my Jugnu Rani so sad today?"

"Suraj Dada," Jugnu said, **"everyone is doing something for Mother Nature. But I am so small that I can't do anything at all. What should I do? Please help me".**

Suraj Dada saw how much Jugnu wanted to do something good. He said to her: "It does not matter how big or small you are. What you need is the will and determination to do

things, and to do whatever you can, with all the strength that you have. Look at me! **I burn in this fire alone, and light up the whole world.** I feel good that my light gives new life to People, Trees and all other beings. Though I am alone, I make Nature and the entire world happy."

Touched by Suraj Dada's words, Jugnu said "Suraj Dada, you are so clever that all the praises for you are not enough... I'm only a little Firefly, but I would also love to do something like you, for our world."

Suraj Dada said wisely, "**Jugnu, you should first travel the world, and understand it...learn from it**. If you don't find something useful by yourself, then come back to me. I will happily show you how to help Mother Nature."

Taking his advice, Jugnu flew off without a second thought.

The beautiful Mehrauli island

Jugnu flew all the way to Mehrauli, a tiny island in a long and wide river. Everyone—Animals, Flowers, Birds, and Insects, Plants, Trees and People—came here for holidays and enjoyed themselves.

The air was cool and everything was in bloom that day. Everyone was busy preparing for the spring festival of Basant. Later, it would be time for the annual Friendship-Meal.

कुमार

A group of People and Trees prepared a meal of tasty dishes from different parts of the world. Everyone shared the tasks and helped each other.

Jugnu felt very happy to see the warm companionship between People and Trees. She was invited to join in for the Friendship-Meal. Soon, everyone was sitting together to eat. The food was so delicious that no one wanted to stop eating!

Jugnu and the Ants

A little while later, Jugnu saw a colony of Ants walking in a neat and orderly line. Not one was out of step from the other. She was not sure what they were doing, so she kept watching them. She saw that each one of them was picking up leftover bits-and-pieces of food from the ground and carrying them away.

She asked them, "Are you going to take away all these leftovers?"

One Ant replied, "No! **We'll take only as much as we need and only as much as we have the strength to carry**. We never take more."

"But why do all of you walk in a single line?" asked Jugnu.

"We are very disciplined," said the Ant. Another Ant spoke wisely, "We have a rule that whenever an ant wants to go out for work, all the other ants will go along to help. Working together makes the task easier. Our time is also spent pleasantly. This is why ants live in one colony."

The ants' words boosted Jugnu's confidence! She began to think happily, "I should also do something useful like this. Look at the ants. By picking leftovers they help clean the surroundings, while they also live together and support each other. **Every living being is doing something for the good of the Earth.**"

Trees stop being friends with People

Everyone was preparing to go home after the Friendship-Meal. People packed up their things and hung them on the branches of Trees. Thoughtlessly, they also put their little children on the branches.

Now the Trees began to feel very heavy with all the weight. It was just too much and they felt unable to cope... Their branches started to bend. It became difficult for them to even walk properly. They were stumbling along slowly, without complaining or saying anything.

When one of the People saw the Trees, he burst out laughing. At this, others also began to laugh. The Trees were unsteady; their branches heavy with things, and here were People laughing at them!

Trees became upset when their friends began to laugh. They felt ridiculed and thought, "Is this what we get in return from People after all that we have shared? Have they forgotten our friendship, care, and helpfulness? We couldn't have imagined such treatment from friends even in our dreams..."

Big drops of tears began to fall from the eyes of the Trees.

They decided at that very moment: they would no longer do anything that People wanted them to do. "We will not speak to them and we will not go anywhere with them," they said.

And then, all the Trees became still.

They kept standing in one place and, slowly, their feet dug into the ground around them. Those feet spread and turned into roots.

Jugnu was very upset at the turn of events. She wished People had not treated Trees so badly. She watched them helplessly.

People say 'Sorry'

Now all the Trees and their children—the Plants—were still. They did not move. People realised that they had made a huge mistake. Without the friendship of Trees and Plants, everything would feel lifeless. Who would be their friends now?

One man said to a Tree, "Dear friend, we were so absorbed in the fun and pleasure of the meal that we forgot the difference between good and bad." He held his hand and pleaded, "Please, please forgive us friend... let us be together again. Without your friendship and support, we will lose our spirit. Life will have no meaning."

But it was too late now. "No," said the Tree, "now we cannot be as we were before. We have made our decision and it is final. We will not change it now."

Jugnu spoke up at this time, "Forgive me friends, I don't mean to interfere. But I agree with the decision taken by this Tree. She has decided correctly."

She turned towards the People and said, "There is a reason why all living beings are put on Earth...our presence here is not for nothing. Of what use are happiness and pleasure if they make someone hard-hearted and cruel? The most intelligent minds on Earth are said to be of People. Now you intelligent People have become selfish and have forgotten your friendship with the Trees. This was not what Mother Nature wanted. She wanted you to live in harmony."

People tried their best to coax the Trees to be friends with them again. They pleaded over and over again, but the Trees were adamant. Finally, when they realized nothing would work, People sat under the Trees and began to repent.

The roots of the Trees—which were once their feet—now went deeper into the soil and sank in the ground. Trees were content and happy, and ate the food that the soil gave them. And because they remained in the same place, they soon became a thick forest!

Jugnu stayed with them all this time. One day, she observed: "Ever since the Trees chose to be fixed to the ground, their branches are filled with small creatures and birds who have made their homes there."

Very soon, the forest was full of many animals, birds, insects and other living beings. Jugnu would roam the forest, fly over the Trees, and feel thrilled to see them all there together.

But, one thought had not yet left her: **"If only I could do something useful".**

A fire in the forest

One night, a great fire suddenly broke out in the forest. Everything was crackling and burning. Jugnu flew out of the forest to get help. She saw the small Bird carrying water from the nearby river in its little beak, and throwing it on the fire. Jugnu asked in surprise, "Little friend, do you really think this tiny amount of water will help put out those tall, wild flames?"

Huffing-and-puffing the Bird replied, "Jugnu, I have no idea if I can put out the fire or not. But this forest is my home. I have to do everything I can to protect it. Some fellow birds might see me doing this and will get inspired to join me." Saying this, off flew the little Bird to fetch more water.

Very soon, Jugnu noticed many more Birds coming to help the little Bird. They went

to the river, filled their small beaks with as much water as they could, then brought it back and threw it on the flames. They did this again and again.

Other animals also joined them, and soon there were Monkeys, Elephants, People and other creatures that came together to put the fire out.

In the darkness of the night, the bright fire-flames became high, lighting up everything. You could see the shadows of People, Animals and Birds, working hard together to put the fire out. Their efforts succeeded! Finally, the flames were conquered and the fire was banished.

Looking around her, Jugnu saw that more than half the forest was burnt down. She thought: "The forest caught fire at night. Had it been daytime, the damage would have been less. It is more difficult for Animals to escape from the forest in the dark. This is why it took much longer to control the fire. **If only it had not been so dark...**"

Jugnu Rani gets Light

After the next day, it was night again. In that dark night, with only a few stars shining in the sky, the pale moon was throwing a weak light on Earth. Jugnu thought to herself, "Millions of stars and in between them is Chanda Mama, the moon. Even they are not able to wipe away the darkness. Only Suraj Dada is able to... all by himself".

"I should do something and protect the animals." Thinking this, Jugnu decided to find a way to put out darkness. She prayed hard to Mother Nature to show her a way to do this. Everyone saw how sincere she was. Mother Nature—the mother of all Trees, People, Animals and Insects—was pleased that her little Jugnu had finally found her purpose to be useful to the Earth and to Environment.

Suddenly, a ray of light burst out of Jugnu's body. It flickered on and went off, and kept flickering on–off continuously. It became stronger and brighter until Jugnu looked like there was a light bulb inside her!

She was transforming into a sparkling Firefly. She was bursting with happiness, and when she looked up she saw the bright Suraj Dada smiling at her from the sky. He had kept his promise! Jugnu had traveled the world and gained many experiences and she had discovered her purpose to be useful, all on her own.

When other Fireflies saw the shimmering Jugnu they also wanted to be like her. They asked Suraj Dada for help and then joined Jugnu.

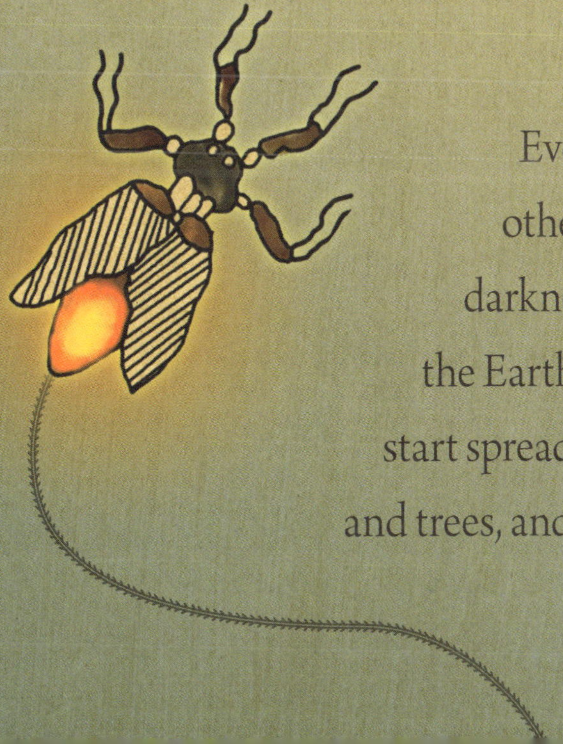

Every day, Jugnu and the other Fireflies keep fighting darkness. As night falls upon the Earth, they get together and start spreading light over forest and trees, and on farms and fields.

First published in India in 2012 by
Mapin Publishing Pvt Ltd
502 Paritosh, Near Darpana Academy,
Usmanpura Riverside, Ahmedabad 380013
T: 91 79 4022 8228 • F: 91 79 4022 8201
E: mapin@mapinpub.com • www.mapinpub.com

Simultaneously published in the
United States of America in 2012 by
Grantha Corporation
77 Daniele Drive, Hidden Meadows
Ocean Township, NJ 07712
E: mapin@mapinpub.com

Distributors
North America:
Antique Collectors' Club
T: 1 800 252 5231 • E: info@antiquecc.com
www.antiquecollectorsclub.com

UK and Europe:
Gazelle Book Service Ltd
T: 44 1524 68765 • F: 44 1524 63232
E: sales@gazellebooks.co.uk

Distributed in the rest of the world by
Mapin Publishing Pvt Ltd

ISBN: 978-81-89995-34-8 (Mapin) pb
ISBN: 978-1-935677-25-3 (Grantha) pb
LCCN: 2010932794

Book and Cover Design: Gopal Limbad/Mapin Design Studio
Editor: Vinutha Mallya/Mapin Editorial

The publishers thank Minhazz Majumdar for her support.

Printed in India by Aegean Offset Printers, New Delhi